I0821616

Other Poetry Books by Norm Sibum

Banjo, 1972

Small Commerce, 1978

Loyal and Unholy Hours, 1980

Beggars, 1981

Among Other Howls in the Storm, 1982

Ten Poems, 1985

Eight Poems, 1987

Café Poems, 1988

Narratives and Continuations, 1990

In Laban's Field, 1993

The Apostle's Secretary, 1993

Septimius Felton, 1994

CD Poets 2, 1995

The November Propertius, 1998

Girls and Handsome Dogs

Norm Sibum

The Porcupine's Quill

NATIONAL LIBRARY OF CANADA
CATALOGUING IN PUBLICATION DATA

Sibum, Norm, 1947–
Girls and handsome dogs

Poems.

ISBN 0-88984-230-2

I. Title.

PS8587.I228G57 2002 C811'.54 C2002-900087-4
PR9199.3.S5173G57 2002

1 2 3 • 04 03 02

Published by The Porcupine's Quill
68 Main Street, Erin, Ontario NOB 1TO
www.sentex.net/~pql

Readied for the press by Eric Ormsby; copy edited by Doris Cowan.
Typeset in Minion, printed on Zephyr Antique laid,
and bound at The Porcupine's Quill Inc.

All interior art is by Mary Harman.

Represented in Canada by the Literary Press Group.
Trade orders are available from General Distribution Services.

We acknowledge the support of the Ontario Arts Council,
and the Canada Council for the Arts for our publishing program.
The financial support of the Government of Canada
through the Book Publishing Industry Development Program
is also gratefully acknowledged.

Canada

Table of Contents

The Inspiration

Redhead with big brown eyes
And a certain sex appeal,
Nobody's fool, everyone's pal, popular here,
a waitress,

It just now hits me how you have
Insinuated your loneliness,
Your desperation and bravado
into my material.

Shall we make it official then and I put to work
A breezy, amatory measure, some equivalent of
Ovid's rising six, falling five,
And get thee in a garter belt
and me from out of my straitjacket?

Oh, just be my muse, my coach, my guide,
And I'll reserve a page, maybe two
Such a deal!
For your cavernous dimple
In this my book of genius.

I Went Out West

The woods in Massachusetts might thaw in the spring
And robins hop over the ground,
And girls and boys link arms and sing
And the old suspect gladness in the first flowers.
The sun, bearing down on Rome, might make her
Too warm and evil, inhospitable to virtue.
It might blister the wastes of old Persia and
Bake to imperishable hardness
Poems from time out of mind,
But men, muttering anywhere, shine –
Inside their bowl of sky –
The dull gleam of the propitiation
Of well-being. Even so, I shivered
As my prayers settled on my bones.

*

I left behind some stockade.
I burdened animals, followed rivers.
The winters snapped at soul and limb.
Men stamped their feet next to the campfires
Far from their fathers' realms
On account of the brutal cold.
How did I keep going?
To whom did I pray?
We penetrated deeper.
Spring once more and the blooms again
Began to article the clouds for spirit
And flesh and manageable truth.

– Solitude was the god. The god, one day,
Would come like a pleasant evening
To bless many a civil scene,
Many a stoop and veranda.
Or, ghost-ship, it would drift
On the seas of the ever-changing.
It'd be a strange land, this,
Always fair for the dead.

Crossword and Storm

She has always known that more is better,
To always be happy the optimum life.
She has always known her dead go to heaven,
But where are they who lived in the house?
She always knew that of love and lust
One is the hunger and one has the force.
Rain pelts the leaves – a squall from the west
Pastes the verdure against the window.
Will she now name the 'Rural Muse' poet,
Pencil the result in crossword squares?
The earth, the stone, the grass,
Cows, maples, the silent tractor,
All of that hill beyond the ditch,
All of the world rise to a storm.

: :

It's a thin teacup.
A thin tea-plate.
It's a large, but dainty, self-sufficient hand.

Milk. Two sugars. *Oh, make it three.*

Shoulders stooped, breasts bunched together,
Hair long and wound, she's loved, unloved,
Adored, and on a better day, humoured.
In the heart of an act as deliberate as this:
Sweetening and whitening the tea, one pushes
One's little fate along.
Consolation.
Lunacy.

: :

It's like a round pale moon in a once stormy sky –
That clock in its casket, timepiece that died.
Still, it keeps the hour, its face unmoved,
Hands frozen to an epiphany.
She used to say, her eyes smarting
From her five winters of the loss,
Old tick-tock, your heart broke
And God the Repairman
Did not come to this house.

: :

There's no word for betrayal in the insect empires, the heirloom of a clock
Silent on the subject.
Rain drips from a leaf, and that same rain
Tips the leaf below –
                    time smells of mice and rotted boards.
In so many ways one tells untruths: by omissions, by pretending
  to truths one lacks, embellishment there
    in the deep, perpetual solitudes.

The mind is intricate because in it
Birds of love and birds of lust
  mix feathers, the urge to honesty an urge like others.
Ominous thunder. Ricocheting thunder.
Shapes in the rain falling now in gusts
Sweep the road and die in the grass.
Is not the heart a thing of bird skin, feathers plucked?
A crash overhead. Lightning splits the air.

: :

Her love for her dead had failed to stand
  the dead their surety – it had not spared them the icy cosmos.
Tears well up. Delicate spasms.
She sucks sweet breath down her throat.
She'll have nothing change in a house of cobwebs.
She won't sweep the floor or take out the trash or wash the dishes
For a while. She may, instead, flee her saintliness
As when, two weeks and a day in a distant place,
She caught up with the human tribe.
The storm veers off – its surly visage
Now meditates on the other hills.
A rift in the cloud. Blue.

*

And she is beautiful and she is calm
As when one occasions no false moves.
And though the clock keeps but imagined time,
And though the crossword is blank, her mind impugned,
Her heart beats strong – her pulse is steady.
She's more than a match for the scent of the grass
And the sharp stone gleaming out there.

A Theme for a Saturday Afternoon

While I lay there, my eyes shut,
Some rose burgeoning in my skull,
I resolved to sniff that flower
For its being the emblem of my desire,
Politics, perhaps, a better subject.
Are not rebellions sacred, peasants noble?
Are not the pitchforks blessed?
Does not the divine instruct
Order on this homely earth?

Her pleasure was swiftly had – she did not linger.

While I lay there, eyes unshut
With which I doodled in the dark,
Tannenbaum rolled a fabric up her legs.
Time and space knit together.
While I saw Berlin, Vienna,
Rome and Manhattan in my mind,
It was prayer: the woman deep in it at the mirror,
Combing silence into her hair.

And while fallen princes pawned their jewels,
While poor men burned their books for fuel –
While weary women boiled cabbages in rusted pots
And whacked their kids, Tannenbaum before her image,
With ivory comb was gathering
God's chaotic pensiveness.
And whole worlds may fall apart
And still, a woman may turn on her heel
And pass beyond a curtain
To the relics that she markets.
Yes! With an air of one for whom
The wolf is always at the door.
I went out that portal to another door.

‘Well, Eddie,’ I addressed the parrot
Who was a picture on the café wall,
Who with beady eye and wicked beak
Looked half the face of God,
‘Did you ever read Hobbes’s Thucydides?’

It should come as no surprise at all
That in the time it takes to blink an eye
Heavens, earths and underworlds
May all rear up and roar
Their arrival on the scene:
Messalina entered Lucky’s Diner.
I could not help but notice her.

Once I read history for the knowledge – now I read it for the smut,
But this darling didn’t resemble a wife of Caesar,
Didn’t seem an habitué of the baths.
Not she who schemed against
Her husband’s speech impediments,
But this Messalina of these avaricious times,
This piece of work chimed like a bell.
Her voice was as pious as a monk’s cassock
With the idea of island heat and cresting wave and a proper man.
‘My kind of girl,’ some old soldier bragged.
I saluted a cackling bird and left.

Sex and Tannenbaum were my theme,
  History a secondary option, religion a distant third …

But now, in a room of the Traymore Rooms –
The year come around to high summer,
Shadows creeping down the terraces
Of moody trees – I reconsider.
While children shriek and dogs romp,
While the old on benches part their lips
To the traces of a breeze, time's the mystery,
Time is the spectre that shakes out her hair and the heart stops.

Ordinary Time

Officer, this morning when I woke up
And threw my feet out of bed
And they too quickly met the floor
And it was a beginning or an end,
To help them regain their poise, I said,

'Noble once, grotesque now, feet of mine,
Convey to the plain, to the confusions,
To the klaxon noise
Of everyday human commerce,
The genius you support.'

Officer, I talked it up, optimist, one who stares down daily
The nine states of exile there are
For each virtue and every vice.
'I'll forgive,' I said, 'and I'll forget
That rude and implacable floor.'
Because Berlin returned to Berlin, one day,
And Somewhere in China yields
Not only markets but the graves
Of long dead nomad princes.
Because I admit to my mistakes
                    as when I mistook
Greed for innocence, extinction for our products.

We came, my feet and I, to the romance of the plain.
                                                  We came and saw
There's room to manoeuvre now.
Suddenly I've eyes of wonder
For the beauties in my line of vision:
The flushed cheeks, the shimmering gowns,
The laughter, the loves of the moment!
An orchestra rippled with dances.
Some Napoleon was amorous,
Bivouacked across the river.

Officer, things with us are so routine, so peaceful and agreeable
That, on occasion, one breaks through
To a world like that: unhurried, unstressed, relaxed
Primitive grab of territory.
Hey, easy with the shackles!
Of course, it's a chimera that I, fair-weather optimist, scored.
So I continued to walk among
The faces of pallor in the district.

As I proceeded, as my expert feet
Trod the paths of well-being,
Boys, stylishly and sullenly,
Pounded basketballs on the pavement –
Clouds settled over the city,
Suffocating the trees. March.
Should the sun appear, should the origin of our light
Warm up shivering poet-heroes avenging
The treacheries of old masterworks,
It might dry out the day a little
And merit again begin to rate its prize.
Maybe in two hundred years.

Then I arrived at the barbershop –
Manfred, lunatic, pointed at the deep-backed chair.
'The usual?' he asked. That arm's bored sweep. 'Back and sides?'
That same menace, same hair rinse. Same wine reek.
He's one to watch.

A populace passed by. Depressed parishioners.
Petitioners after rectitude, two-coated buyers of
Purchase one, get the next item free.
Manfred began to snip.

Oh, he grunted, he chuckled. He fibrillated air
Through hairy nostrils. He tilted his head this way, that way, rotated mine.
Was it my politics, my dirty, blond curls?
Was I mad and imperial?

He stood at the window, razor in hand, and stared at the street
For the longest time. There were long-lost ambitions in him.
Then he sidled over to scrape
My cheeks, my chin, my neck.
That same menace, hair rinse, reek of wine.
So worried a Domitian, a Diocletian, a Constantine.

Have you noticed that ten thousand procedures,
Diagnosing one sickness, suggest a million treatments?
Still, the brides leave you as when it's naught but sex one day
And abstinence the next, and they emote
                all the way to the bus stop.
Anyway, shaven, I pressed on, contemptuous, a choirboy's song on my lips,
The whispers in my café, nine kinds of exile and the same old talk
Getting me nowhere. I could not fix
Those dismembered by TV plots.

But I sensed shyness in the girl
Whose hand cupped a mug of beer. Was she half the world
As when the heart beats quicker
At the miracle? Officer, you sneer.
Well, you have your social work – you've tolerances to test.
So when you go do your public relations,
Don't do as I would do: speak forever
Of life and death, whim and art.
I surely meant to pay for breakfast.
Manfred cleaned my purse.

So I said to the woman last night: 'Ditch your boyfriend. Dine with me,
As all the houses are sad, as one must make music.
And we'll cross the plain and we will establish
If these are the best or the worst of times,
And then, brave, say it does not matter.'
It's ordinary time, everyday time, time that harries
Waitresses, bank clerks, cops, adepts of saucepans, calculus,
parliamentary obligations –
Time such as moves one to say,
'Has there not been improvement on the days
When good ladies brought the church alms
And kissed the True Cross?'

Burn rosemary, cypress to purge the air.
Festoon your house with fragrant branches.
Light candles against the dark that is always with us.
Do not flatter it –
Do not deny it, lambs roaring, lions bleating, poets keening like jackals,
Clowns mumbling mass, and men like me
Pleading eccentricity, everyone in on the kill.
Officer, send away the dogs and I'll lodge no complaint
Against you, the cook or the girl. I always make
My restitution.

The Song of Nickles the Artist

I do not know what governs
  Our business in this life.
I suspect a tin god speaks
  For the old sovereignty of chance.
If you must stare, I'll tell you
  The nose, flat thing on my face,
Is pugnacious.
This nose has a nose for beauty
  And sails to loveliness.

Coffee drips into a pot.
  A smell of butter on the toast.
It's as though the bread were fruit,
  Butter the emanation
    Here in the restaurant.
It's as though a longing were
  In these items.

Each morning as I arise
  On my pasha's couch,
I am still dreaming
  The toes of restless virgins.
Stuck on loving the lovely
  That are not beloved,
I have aim: it is to draw
  The digits.

Penny, my misplaced waitress,
  Unacknowledged legislator,
Is neither young nor beautiful –
  I have never drawn her toes.
Still, she'll treat with any bum
  Come to cadge esteem.
Who knows?
Chance may have made us both
  Hungry for a life
Or just something plain
  Ineffable.

In the eyes of Penny
  Is the entire story:
Blondes who are less evolved than Dietrich
  Star in almost everything.
Penny rose from low-life rancour
  To the rank
  Of service industry worker.

Few will ever eavesdrop here
  On a discussion of Schopenhauer.
But I shall attach to Penny
  Such a head of hair
As hasn't topped the hour
  Since the Sun King died
With his curls on.

And she shall wear rough palm leaves
   For a pair of sandals.
And she shall have the moon
   For a diadem.
And she shall secure
   For her whim and for her folly
The prune-wrinkled hearts of men.
And who but I, Nickles,
   Draws the picnic spreads
Of Glamorous Evolution: the lovelies, the bikers,
   The pit bulls, the sunsets?

You die from it –
   You're dead from what's
Sad and sweet and comic.
   Penny tramps
From booth to table
   And back again –
Like a California brush fire,
   Like a fund-raiser.

If there's a heaven and it's permitted
   To love tall and perfect strangers there
Who never break,
   Snap back or irritate,
She'll take the plunge.

And the mirror in the café gleams
    With the late summer green of trees,
The residences,
    The small commerce.
The future gnaws
    On our soft
Inner tissues....

And the posters the mirror reflects
    Call out the vote –
There are violations in the traffic
    And a flight of birds.
Once, a painter's immortality
    Was all that,
Technique,
    Tea leaves,
Pretty birds,

            and the brown eyes of a waitress
and a shade of lipstick
and a shape of earring.

Wintergreen Licentious

I went the way many times
   Along the road to the sea
And with the daughters of the cruelties took
   Old routes to knowledge.
Drinking whisky in the kitchen helped
   For telling the truth to one another.
Grand truths and little ones
   Sufficed for a consensus.
Sylvie said, 'It rains today. It's you I love.'
Fact. Supposition.

And sometimes Mabry met me
   In the old heart of the town.
We'd walk to the rotting harbour
   And smell how a harbour smells.
We'd argue the mystic duty
   Of America to decline.
I'd kiss her cheek and would kiss her body
   But all of her declined.

Sometimes I'd keep a book
   Open to a certain page.
And I would not turn it
   Over the course of a day.
I'd read only those directives
   That post angels to stand guard.
The sun went around the sky –
   The moon bloomed in transit,
Stars scattered seed.

Even so, a daughter of the cruelties
  Would go and hail a taxi.
She would secede from me
  In the way change occurs.
It is as when a wind
  Brushes dune or cloud
Or makes leaves go silver, rearranging the relations
  Between those dreaming and those damned.

But, you know, rather than receive
  Condolence for one's sweet mistakes,
In place of commiseration where
  One's always lost,
You had only to set out,
  Bring pertinacity, bring sails to the wind,
Keep going,
  Give no interviews.

Celia and I lit tiny candles,
  Ate desserts sacred to a goddess.
We gossiped – raucously –
  Of her latest beau.
A sea breeze blew warm and gentle
  On the candle flames.
Musicians in black frocks
  Serenaded on the balcony.

The music said: 'This music is
  An urn of green glass.
It contains love's
  Bones and ashes.
It is women keening
  When they do not laugh.
It is engineering
  As when buildings rise and objects fly,

All the while saying
  That power's the first reality,
Love the sideshow.
So step this way
  Into the mind.'

Like a partridge drunk from feeding
  On soft, autumn apples
I flap (such is my sex)
  From incident to incident.
I conclude there is no other
  More attractive description.
There's the flesh of the corporeal,
  The rag and gas of soul
And then
  The dying pensioners on endless stairs.

This vellum oddment, turn of the century –
  The nymphet in her boots, her sad enthusiasts ... look on it, learn.
Or beat a ground of poets
  For the proper revelation:
Let your gods be stolen, they'll
  Devour you in turn.

And then once the end begins
  To join with a new start,
Or when a new economy
  Cancels moral outlook,
In gratitude one leers – if one is ordinary
  And drinks and whores and resets the wheel.
I have lived like that.

But I must say I never
   Went to bed with Maggs, her eyes a lovely blue.
She was ravishing in her gown
   The night she came to speak her mind.
'Who's Aristotle?' she asked
   And asked for what was in the bottle.

'Wintergreen,
   You unshaped the womb that birthed you!
The heat of the sun and the cold of the moon
   On the road to the sea has weathered you.
There's a morgue – it is this earth –

   There are rumours of better things to come.
But I, I can't go quite as merrily as you
   Along the road of pilgrimage.

'Wintergreen, it is because I wish to have
   My guarantee of an item
Whose nature we debate,
   Whose essence lies in darkness,
Whose passing is rather swift
   From when it declares its presence.
You may kiss my cheek
   And I'll be trundling off.'

I must tell you she, she laughed lightly at herself
   As she ended it, ended
Her little dissertation on the game of love and its intricate
      rules.
Such noble vehicles – taxis,
   So well suited for the leave-taking.

Hypatia

I

I went often to the town
To conduct business in the place
　　With a populace of zealots, with other patriots.
The cows stood in their pastures. Fish swam in trout pools.
The librarian liked her gin, her men,
Her Dashiell Hammett novels. Everyone had weather
Good or bad, the bed & breakfast cedar-shingled
　　In the woods.

II

Shirley at the truck stop, she of a hundred shapes, hefted herself
　　Through village time and space.
'Dear' and 'hon' she said as she served the corn
And brought the sodas
To misdirected tourists,
Those ladies of blue hair,
　　Powder, rouge and substance.

III

A dream used to put me in a sweat.
I'd cower in tall, savanna grass.
As thunder broke above, me whimpering in a tongue,
I counted on my finger
　　My apparent purpose:
Two thousand million years of sun and travellers counselling patience.

IV

I'd wake, my eyes milky in the darkness, the numbers of a clock
    Red, diabolical, digital.
I'd wonder how she did it, the librarian, I mean – how bed down
The realtor, the lineman, the supplier of cords of firewood
    And keep them all in true?
Her soprano laugh? Her figure as unforgiving
    As a plank of two-by-six?

V

I went often to Hypatia, having business there.
I'd say, 'Hey, James!' He was always at the corner.
The indigent in pigtails once drove long-haul,
    The hair getting dingier.
Did I have a fiver? Sure, I had
A note of the realm to spare.

VI

One full moon night, the bushes thick with berries, pines reflecting
    White lunar heat,
I met three immortals at their meal of beef and greens and ginger,
And they were larking and they were solemn
In the Golden Dragon
    By the spiky succulent.

VII

To emulate the administration of good order, one caught – like one catches
colds –
    Sobriety, detachment, chastity.
Sue and Greer were mothers, Babs a gifted amateur
Who could have solaced Socrates
    But had befriended truckers.

VIII

From then on, Sue and Greer and Babs
    Made my evenings honest.
Nothing was as it used to be though even the gardens of the rich
    Breathed pious projects.

IX

And we'd drink and shout and sing old hymns
And beat rhythms with our spoons
    Against pretty, painted cups.
I'd kneel and pray, earth, water, fire and air,
Virtue, too, and knowledge
    Still perennial.

X

One always had business in the town: cheeses to buy, honey to sell,
    Auto parts to deal.
One inspected the library for overweening ambition.
One brought chocolates to the librarian. In the ivy-choked hotel I kept a room.
Well, the world is master, yet speak those words too much
In whimsy, and one's a beast,
    And it's all up with us.

XI

I always threw a party when I came to town, the evenings close, the flowers fleshy,
    Birds edgy in the sky.
A patrician clink of whisky glasses
To the pleasures of the ballroom, to the antics of the bed,
To the figure-ghosted gardens, to the shadow-softened stadiums.
To each and every mystic heart of the land!
Because time that makes immemorial the monuments of pain
    Remembers and defeats us
    And forgets us in the end.

XII

Sometimes they stayed all night, Sue and Greer in sleep
Dreaming what delicate birds dream of things. Babs brooded.
For when the virgin and the angel
Bartered with what they had – he the express desire of heaven,
She the bitter portions of the earth – heaven remained heaven.
    Earth regrettably didn't.

XIII

I often woke at dawn to smell dew on yellow leaves. I'd smell the salt sea.
Damn me if I couldn't smell
The numbers of a clock-machine –
    They glowed like red-hot brands.

XIV

A journalist
Aged fifty-four, frightened now of everything, showed on occasion
    With sacks of beer.
He'd sprawl on the floor, an ingénue, some character of Boccaccio.
He'd stare at the ceiling and charm us
With the rag-ends of his promise
    And the carnage he had seen.

XV

Against the age and aging, with Babs and Sue and Greer and me,
    He was shut in, too.
Even if the moon was full, the birches silver, the fountain on a patch of green
Exuding peace, he'd settle down with us, a box within a box,
    Hope a deadly thing.

XVI

This Edgar thought himself well hidden:
The baseball cap and sneakers, the cult of Pabst Blue Ribbon.
Of Babs, I'd say: those happy now, those peevish now
Inamorata lips! And who, indeed, belonged
To the gleaming white convertible
Parked by the wooden church
        If it wasn't Reverend Creep?

XVII

Sometimes we spiced the question with our special type of humour
Whilst we knocked our spoons
        Against every pretty surface:
'The hand that rocks the cradle, dear …'
'The Bearded Woman!' 'The Paying Customer!'
I fancied a pose Velázquez struck
When he portrayed the court
        And shrugged at God.

XVIII

The imperial agent he is one who pollinates the colony
With a message and a joke, with a summons, with a dispensation.
He gleans taxes, snatches of poems, and he rounds up martyrs
        And plays it by the book.
Babs has slept with him –
        On principle. She owed much.

XIX

James once drove long-haul – to Trenton and Tallahassee.
Edgar traded in events. Sue was big, not svelte, Greer red-haired, small.
Babs, resident theologian, called a storm-black sky
A vast black rebuke, spread across her lap
        The pages of a work
Squeezed from joy and agony,
        Composed by John in Ephesus.

XX

Edgar, a gentleman, was all rank and file, his hands – like crumpled
                                                                spiders – resting
On a six-pack. We'd send out James for smokes.
Condemn the times and one deserves
        To be deemed an amateur.

XXI

Maybe it was the whisky, maybe the redhead snoring
Beside me on the bed. Maybe it was the sight of Babs
Waiting for dawn to light the room, her lips slow-dancing
To a lazy chanson. What does one do with holiness?
        I'd close my eyes, try to sleep.

XXII

A bird in the room – a parrot. It flew around the room
In which Babs sat, concubine of the Lord.
It said *AWK!* It said *Sin! Futility!*
Over and over. And it was as though some old master
Had painted Babs from memory, her nose aquiline,
Eyes violet in the smoke of cigarettes
  She imagined was religious.

XXIII

At heart, passion's like that, splendid and nervous
  What with the green feathers.

XXIV

One always had business in Hypatia, the weather moving fast
Through the wind-raw skies over the cyclone-breeding ocean.
The towering clouds came ashore
The other side of those Main Street blinds
And menaced the orchards there, the motley lands,
The broken fences everywhere
  Of captives of the spirit.

XXV

I was just a poet in the constable's report, merry and inadmissible,
No fixed address, no rigged doctorate
  Backing the majesty of the mind.
I gave my name as Phemius, a bard whose pretty throat
Was keen to avoid the business edge
  Of a warlord's hunting knife.

XXVI

One came to Hypatia, revolution in one's heart, and met with friends
And caught their luck. You sat in kitchens – you drank too much
While a girl shot full of pessimism
    Leaned against the door.

XXVII

A cartoonist now, you drew seven dancing monkeys
So as to entertain her, so as to undress her, so as to kiss
Her jaded loins. The merry creatures
Tipped their hats and twirled their canes.
A toe-happy chorus, it'll sing straight-faced, for all time, to God.
One always had business like that in the town,
    The baths steaming, the buses efficient.

XXVIII

I do think of Shirley, the way she moved and talked in time and space,
Was selfish, was blind with cause, oblivious of effect.
The way red lacquer shone on her nails.
    James was always snake-bit.
The librarian had her gin, her beet-red face, her consorts,
    And Dashiell Hammett.

XXIX

Sue and Greer, virtuous, lecherous, fickle, constant,
Dreamed like birds on holidays, the truckers and the farmers
    Scuffling on their bones.
Babs worked it out: redemption a glittering ballroom.
Edgar flamed
    In an auto crash.

XXX

One always had business in Hypatia even when one stayed away.
It'd been grim, overly touted: lovers attached by beads of fluid,
Meteors drowning in the sky
    On late summer nights.

XXXI

Still, one could admire the roses,
Could walk around and scatter the leaves,
Breathe the salt from off the sea, smell a storm
    Approaching.

XXXII

And one could say: *And some were brave and some were gentle*
And some were cruel, coming all that way. And there came a time,
The land settled, the bullets moulded, the dance bands jiving, the poetry thick,
The question 'How are we doing?' spiritual,
When – through one's relations to the mysteries
In all the temples of love – one got smashed to bits.

Girls and Handsome Dogs

The time went by in the afternoon, the rosy cumulus
an invasion force.
Gleaming cars reflected the shady streets.
And girls and handsome dogs
High-stepped on the avenues.
Came the rain, the just and the fatuous
And the experts in all the pleasures
Took cover, voices harp-like
As in a dream. I do not know if we are forever marching
toward our capture
Or toward release
But light glowered as light will do
In holy places. It rained a while on marigolds,
Temples sliding into the sea.

: :

Let's just say it stormed and then
A cloud was spent. The sun shone again
On maples, steamy verandas.
Girls and handsome dogs
High-stepped on the avenues.
That people always find
Their declarations convenient: 'It's wet.' 'It's hot.'
'The dead have risen....'

– It was like a gardener's hand
Rooting around in earth, time's touch – like a pensive lover's
careless hand
That, in passing, brushes blooms.
There had been that filthy cloud, the humidity.
The demands of nature and of pleasure eat
at all veneers.
The time went by in the afternoon
As I picked up a stick and drew.
Stars, moons, Arabs, camels, Allah.
Who knows why these comic shades
Of the absolute?

: :

Now, just at sunset, I go, the sky blue-black and deepening
Over a metropolis of hot-tar rooftops
and copper domes.
At the last light I'm on my way
With bravado born of craving – to Delia's
Past lindens and dahlias and the old
On their constitutionals, those old of critical eye.
Is it with me so obvious?

Summer, and one ought to make
The season good with Delia. I'm on my way
From a room light enough. I know nothing
Of man, woman, child
Who live and die – I'm on my way
To a table set with elegance, to daisies fresh from the countryside,
To candles and wine.
The wind warm.
The beetle shiny.
Birds riotous.

To meet my addled heart I go, am in transit
to an amorous spoor.
By time's touch pushed along,
My lazy progress
Hastens. And even that flower in its box,
A bird on its stalk, blooms
With just the right hint
Of concupiscence.

*

Because all that eat
Seek to exploit – by hand, by claw,
by beak, by tooth –
All that must eat know anxiousness.
To love is to go hungry and it is to banquet.
I will sit at the Delia-table and be stroked –
I'll rise up on my hind legs, beseech – I'll beg for
my portion.

Indeed, the sky deepens
To the deep stars everywhere, I anticipating
Delia's cucumber soup, Delia's passion for baroque strings.
Already there's a catch in my throat
Such as too lovely an evening might bring.

Young Love

Dunstan went to see Iris dear.
She was Homecoming Queen in her glory days.
The sky above a town of grain towers
Was always angry (which is why she left the area).
It was the hour for a plebeian ale,
For lighting cigarettes and dangling wrists,
For reclining like a pair of Romans,
Imaginary slaves dancing to imaginary flutes.
Was there ever any innocence to have lost?

It was the hour for disclosing all things,
Even the origins of one's sins.
It was the hour for the qualities
Of what never was and never can be.

*

A phantom lover saw to her needs.
Iris half-dozed on a ratty couch.
Dunstan, disconsolate, sipped a beer.
He stared at her mooning eyelids.
What had she said, this sphinx, this sybil
At the stark commencement of the affair?
'John the Baptist lived off the terrain –
Jesus Christ dined out.'

*

The room was her realm and splendour and prison.
A rose-red umbrella gave shade to a mat.
But it hadn't rained for five days and a week –
Iris had swatted the air with a fan.

Dunstan would sit without clothes on,
Impudent echo of some master scheme.
We live in the day and for the day –
Can't be anything wrong in that.

*

So American it was, so informal and free
That it seemed to Dunstan that Iris and he
Were surrounded by trios born to music,
That wheezed on harmonicas and slapped thighs.
It was the hour to exchange chit-chat

Of what never was and never can be
And of death, taxes and the weather.
'If dreams aren't riddles and puns and teasers,
If they don't attach *epi* to phenomenon,
Either they're godsent vexations or
They're the spices in the meatballs.'

'What's that you say, bucko?' Iris stirred.
Her voice, a creamy contralto, filled the air.
Like Theodora, empress of Byzant,
She had been an exotic dancer.
'I said we live for the tidbits that contain
The sceptic in every spiritual nexus.
It's what the stars spin out as their glass creations.'
Iris was blameless, always that way,
The jade plant profiting by her regime,
The geranium an armada of red sails.

*

A gown clung to Iris's tall frame.
Gloves made elegant her slender arms.
A can of beer on the broken floor
Stood near her reach, her thirst half-quenched.
Dunstan looked at the ceiling, saw God
Or something like God. He shivered.
Iris grinned.

*

A phantom lover had seen to the woman.
She half-dreamed with a drowsy look.
Dunstan wriggled out of her clutches.
The embrace had admitted him more than it loved him.
A hand of solitaire was spread on the table.
A Cleveland Bible lay open to Acts.
'We'll drive to St Louis, pretend it Damascus,'
Iris said when they had first met.
Could he, a beau-designate, vouch
For a god's godly ramble on the earth?
Could he? By the heat in his crotch?
By that bead of delicious sweat on her lip?
By the sight of some bird flayed in a ditch?
By the paradox of a coin standing on its edge?
By the thought that his thought would forever plummet
Through the wide heart of the universe?

*

Iris, sitting up now
In her rumpled gown with green, organza bow,
Used to drift up and down the coasts,
And in the bars read Aeschylus.
She tired of the performance.
'I'd shimmy,' she said, 'and shake
Not only from too much liquor,
From the clammy eyes of bad-smelling drunks,
But from the praises, that in my heart,
I heaped on Abraham Lincoln.'
They stood now in the room's exact centre,
Two tall bodies of equal stature,
She tittering, he searching for her mouth.
It was modest behind her gloved hand.
'Until next time?' Dunstan promised.
'Until next time,' Iris whispered.
She led him to the door with expedition
And sent a fool, hopeless, into love.

Aginthorpe on the Divan

A Bash at Aginthorpe's

Aginthorpe threw a party –
  A slew of people came

Perhaps for no other reason
  But that they were alone
In a crowd, in a marriage,
  In a frivolous game – perhaps for no earthly good reason
But that time remained
    the sum of their days.

: :

Venus, Bacchus, Priapus once
  Presided over every little get-together.
Now professionals shove you pills –
  The mumbo jumbo sends you packing. There are your
    girdle, vine and staff –
There are your stolen moments pinched
    from home and office.

: :

In the way some women stop by the café
  To grab a coffee and cigarette, to complain of the dog,
Of the father, the husband, the son,
  Before attending evening services,
So Mrs D showed at Aginthorpe's –
  Was hard-nosed and friendly,
Her loneliness nothing she couldn't handle,
  Her eyes made up for communion.

: :

And there was Aginthorpe bending
  The psyches of the middle-aged
All tender and vulnerable, all taxed to death. And there he was, so to speak,
  In velveteen, twirling the ends of his moustache,
High on the hill where the air's more pleasant
  Than the miasma of the malarial plains.

: :

There he was, like the poet Mallarmé –
  Just wind him up and he'd instruct,
Something green in his glass,
  Elbow propped on top of the fireplace.
There he was conscientiously trying to seize
    a classic notion: how the soul is one of nature's jests,
  We the thing that makes it miserable.

All these prodigals come home to mother,
  These faint of heart still insisting
Reality's only a construct … well,
  The eyes don't deceive – the heart is the trick.

: :

What with Sinatra, what with the drinks,
  The cushioning and only sometimes frightful
Spectre of sex, it was a quorum.
How the guests laughed, how the guests shrieked,
  How they thought, 'God, what an idiot!'
The moon was full. The night was cold.
Aginthorpe went from room to room
    like Marco Polo.

And the strangest sight he came across,
  As weird as one-eyed men and one-footed freaks,
As bizarre as every human monster seemed
  To the titillated medieval mind,
Was the immeasurable weight of belief
  And the wafer-thin ice on which it rested.
Mariott on the couch,
  Weighing in at three hundred pounds,
Rammed his intelligence into the evening,
  His smile that of a secret lover.
The size of his brain, the circumference of each his thighs
  Mocked every decency, *the economy a cat in heat.*

: :

As Aginthorpe went around,
  As a welcome hung to his face
By a sliver of cheer, that mention of *fluminum amores* he heard
    struck him as a fluke.
As Aginthorpe passed from face to face,
  Looking for an honest decadent, he rated some uttered prurience
By its capacity to unhinge a jaw.
Now and then a joke did cast aspersions
  On every high office – the bravado stretched itself so very thick
Across the frontiers of art and science.
A virgin expanse of greed
  Was the tenebrous shadow of the White House.
The warmer the slander, the hotter the market …

: :

Aginthorpe shrugged, that is, if one can be said to shrug
While hurtling in a cocoon of night
Through the nightmare of a space
doubling on itself –
As though in that maelstrom one could find
One's Egypt,
One's concubine and drug,
A desert spread out like a blanket,
Pyramids prayerful, somnolent

– the world awfully sacred –

A woman in a Chinese hat looked
interesting.

: :

Her headgear a thing of brocade and silk,
Her eyes powder-filled capsules each
Of unwarranted hope and obnoxious confidence,
the woman said, 'Ah, the lord of the castle,
War-monger, tithe-gatherer.'

– She curled her toes inside her brogues
and rocked on the balls of her feet –

Aginthorpe said, 'Few people, if any, of any era
Thought virtue empty, fame hollow –
That fortune conducts the music,
The tonal quality of which
Is the tin a can echoes with
when one boots it.'

– The woman blinked, she a little tense –

She said, 'Well, I've no idea – I haven't the foggiest
As to what you could possibly be on about.
Destiny is a word that begins with *d.*
I like men I can bounce off walls.
A resistance deep in the heart of the game
We call identity, perpetuation
(over and against empire and love),
I was born to rewrite the rules.'

Aginthorpe responded (like a man on the street
observing passing pageantry),
'There's whisky in the kitchen, snacks, hors d'oeuvres,
And cannon fodder for the cause.
In that desk, right-hand drawer, you'll find
Candles, maps, communiqués,
A calf-bound book of lyrics,
All of which when brought together
May magically induce,
If not the Truman Library,
Then the Essene-like atmosphere
of Mao's caves.'

– Aginthorpe could hold out for a day or two yet,
on the fat of his body, at the discretion of his soul –

: :

Aginthorpe sniffed at each compelling group,
Heard:
'Life? Don't have a life – wouldn't know what life is
if it bit my prick.'

Heard:

‘I like a good romantic comedy – I like it when the man’s a rogue,
  The woman shrewd but with the right instincts,
Her channels open to the life-force.’

Heard:

‘That being said, the effect, I think, of a century’s worth
    of gratuitous horror
  Is that humankind, in its wisdom, begins to select
For a sensibility devoid of art,
  Rank sentimentalism the labour,
    sanctimony the signature key.’

    – Mariott had proclaimed,
        his double chin gone still –

Heard:

‘In our numbers, in our loose tandems
  With one another’s grotty lives,
We might constitute a cult,
  The eerie images of which
Are worked in creamy wax,
    a mural of Rome’s Fourth Style.’

    – Aginthorpe had sung for his supper,
        his sad eyes at home with the grotesque pride of the world –

: :

Now in the kitchen Aginthorpe sampled
    this aggregate....

For starters, Frank had killed a man, maybe two, maybe three –
  Sooner or later, he'd do it again.
Tammy diSica wanted a house in the 'burbs
  And it was she that Frank was poking.
Now Oriole debated old Peter and argued him down
  On the virtues of some archaic socialism –
And the wrinkled and sullen Pan
  Whom she addressed, like Khrushchev banging his shoe,
Pounded the table with a mug of beer.
Squinty-eyed Peter, loose in the jowls,
  Some far descendant of Genghis Khan,
Spat and said,
  'Pah! Poetry is useless
    but I tolerate it in women.'

: :

There was snow on the balcony, moonlight in the trees.
There were people in Aginthorpe's house
  Who were devout and who were sincere.
It was heard: 'Come see, daddy. Come see. Come see.'
What? Had someone brought kids
  To this debauch, piss-up, hoedown, orgy?

: :

And either Aginthorpe would open his eyes
  And to them subjoin the darkness,
Or, some night, he'd slip away into sleep
  Like a swimmer in reverse,
That is, like a fugitive ducking under
    so as to come up for air.
But here was the Turcotte woman
  Laughing her sweet vengeance
    into the eyes of Aginthorpe.

: :

Oh, she brought the scene a touch of class.
She was always elegant, always
  Touchingly provincial. Her contralto delivery
Carried all before it – it conveyed her essence
  Through a time and space continuum
    of erotic possibility.
Aginthorpe knew giddiness –
  Something was tumbling
    in his stomach.

    – Knees buckled. His mouth flew open –

'Hello,' he said.
'Hello,' she said, laughing eyes gone neutral
    as in a brush-off.
Priscilla – her daughter – stood beside her
    in oversized denims.

    – Aginthorpe drifted far away
      to an ancient place, to its lulling heat –

: :

Where, on the road out of town one could pass
  Gaudy temples, tombs, lush gardens.
Where, on the road out of town one could see
  The priests and the priestesses.
You could see them in their bright sheer fabrics,
  See them dozing on the steps of each love-pagoda,
See them sated with the ritual sex,
  Numb from the constant mewing
    of lullabies.

: :

'Stay,' said Aginthorpe when the hour got late,
   When certain ladies, as a unit, rose to leave –
When certain men, loud and drunk and sullen,
   Refused to go –
When smiling and mischievous,
   The good ladies bent down
To kiss their host goodnight –
He lay now on his divan.
'Stay,' said Aginthorpe, 'we'll loosen knots
      and solve mysteries.'

      – What better excuse to give
         to keep an occasion alive? –

Going out the door, those ladies were like simple birds
   Fleeing simple dangers in an explosion of wings,
Aginthorpe's smile a full-blooded
   Classical dialogue, an emblem, however faded,
      of dignity.

Light will not return to its star –
   Love will not find the beginning again.

      – His turn to sigh, he fell
         into a fathomless sleep –

To –

When you depart for the new seat of empire
Over the island-tormented sea,

When you leave for those seven hills
And the rude forts and villas

(for surely, it's finished here),
Take with you something to remind you of
our ancient groves.

Go then
but without guilt or shame or sense of failure

To bedevil the going –
eternity is but a brief duration.

Though men might contend with men and build
A romance of endeavour

And houses in which to contemplate it,
Who will quarrel with passing time –

Who will mince words with the decay
That paints us all with its breath?

Now don't fuss too much in your choice of memento –
Most anything will do:

A brooch, a jar, a ritual knife,
a passage by Livy,

For where you go
both god and man –

Shining anew, star-crossed – are militant
And not inclined to leisure.

Bedtime Stories

You know how it is in certain dreams:
  Events are self-evident – there are intimations and yet
You can't say who she is, why she's in your bed,
  And why she's so eager, all of a sudden, hot for you.
The interrogation goes like this:

Man, speak up! Is she fond or isn't she
  Of ruffled green blouses, of glass slippers,
Of diamonds and amethysts, rubies and such,
  Of earrings that, as they dangle, imitate birds?
Does she live around here?

    – But you won't be bullied. You won't be pushed around
      by a collective bored out of its skull –

Her politics now?
                    You haven't a clue.

Fantasies?
              You're in the dark there, too.

Hardly the prince
  She's come to rely on most,
You'll volunteer, however, that her thin ankles are
  The pillars of your sensory world,
But that you're only
                    her plan B, Your Honours,

Her almost Johnny-on-the-spot
  At the Casanova Club, at the Café Zanzibar,
    at the Purple Onion.

: :

You know how it is in certain dreams:
  They move beyond the point of no return.
You're going to sink, drop from the sky. You're going to burn
  As the Reichstag did when it was torched –
And the one in the bed beside you,
  Double-agent,
Her breasts like ripe avocados,
  She's an old, judgemental crone
Though she laughs clearly and purely at you –
  Like any high-minded girl.

: :

You know how it is with these dreams –
  They come at you like the wind,
And they'll blow the door shut on every truth,
  And you'll be the thing you've always been,
Frozen in the quaint dream-crystal of sooty air
    and wintry streets,
That you'll be knocked about
  By the gonging of cathedral bells.
You're the pimply clown, aren't you,
    the consumptive who thought Berlin was bad,
  Who couldn't get any sex?

Wife of the Lamb of the Universe

She was lovely to behold, the young woman in blue –
Hair lustrous black, eyes green, mouth bright.

People, on instinct, made way for her,
Her carriage regal, her demeanour serious

On a market day – she
Brooded at her task.

Yes, the grapes she inspected, the lemons and the oranges
More purple now, more yellow and blood-red

Helped construct the pretty riddle
That appetite is love.

Old men more nobly gnarled, their wives less fretful
And so much more serene,

Dancing days behind them, nonetheless, because of the girl,
Were an infectious rhythm.

The young more lusty, the dogs more playful,
Swaddled babies more sweet and promising …

There was cavorting and yelling, sleeping and yelping,
Days infinite.

And the sky was a song as she touched now this apple
And squeezed that plum, considered the strawberries –

All the while she fingered, at her neck, the tiny gold cross
On its chain –

Raised it, pressed it to her lip –
As she smiled, as she showed her white teeth – briefly.

Dawn, with Fetishes

Aginthorpe woke, and the sky was blue

And it was cold – a sceptic's sky, good sky
   For the getting of one's capital.
It was just the sort of sky one needs
   To extend one's power and gain one's shadow,
A winter sun without weight or substance
      in command.

Aginthorpe peered, as it were, into himself, and saw,

One after the other, a president in Dallas,
   A poet in Rome – his face a death mask,
Each dead man somehow able
   To address the chaos at his core

As will the workings of providence, as will poetry
   When it will finally out – sooner or later, even with beauty.

Aginthorpe saw the poet's grave in its pleasant place,

And he amused himself with a pretty thought
   Of tombs, of time, of breezes and flowers –
He heard the braying horns of Roman traffic.

He saw the wife of the president, in blood-splattered pink,

And she was more than mortal in a theatre of stone,
   Cradling in her hands, as though it were a bird,
A portion of her husband's brains.

– 'Destiny's cold bits,' she explained –

Aginthorpe said:

'Pity comes and pity goes
  Whatever the health of a regime.

'And the passions invite and the passions dispel
  Sympathy.

'And some will preach the long-term solution
    and some a quicker fix
To a strange state of affairs
  That we've made our own.
It goes according to no rhyme or reason –
  Talk is silly, action futile, silence unbearable.'

Then Aginthorpe's phone rang –
  Here was a person of jaundiced persuasion:

Blah blah blah

And she distrusted love
  Or that which had beset her again.

: :

A winter sun without weight or substance
  Lit the window of the bedroom.
The upright twigs of a boulevard tree –
  Like the ribs of a birdcage turned on end –
Formed a bowl of desire – Aginthorpe watched it
    sway in the breeze.
A winter sun without weight or substance
  Was some aggressive thing
Putting out its creeping roots,
  Grabbing fistfuls of corruption.

    – Dream state? Waking state? Who knew any more? –

Well, was he married with children and did the government have
  The most part of his wages?
Had he sired Clever, Smirk and Smug,
  The one a poet, the second a critic,
The third your average soul, a con?
Could he not perhaps get a group rate
    at some altar of sacrifice?

If everyone seemed to have a convenient god,
  Where was his?

What, was he some Ishmael-like figure
  Cast out from the ballroom?
Was he to be escorted from the killing floors
  By trombone-playing marines?

On the other hand, a street of stately elms,
  Of expensively coiffed daughters
    of silver-hair raiders –
It is what stirs Aginthorpe from head to toe –
  It is what tells him where he, a fetishist, belongs,
That is to say, in a first-class coach of the Orient Express,
  On a barstool in the QE II,
In a smoking lounge of the Ritz-Carlton,
    romantic musical segues lilting in him.

Yes, he always preferred to embrace his captor
  And dismiss every unpleasantness.
But would she have him sweet-talk her
  As though he were an outlaw and she his hostage?
Yes, he'd be easy and laugh, 'Where to for breakfast, girl?'
  And she'd answer:
'To Emilio's! For the strawberries and cream,
  For the harsh coffee impossible to sweeten,
For the stack of newspapers
  Rich in gossip of Vienna
And the demimonde of Cleveland –
  For the supercilious air
Of the pickle-nosed waiter Hans.
Let us grow old in some shack by the sea!
But let us not say our arms will be as sieves
  When we grope for one another and reminisce.'

Ablutions

Aginthorpe got up and ran to the bathroom
On the wings of extremity.
Aginthorpe lolled his head at the heavens
And emptied the bag in his side.
Aginthorpe saw in the mirror the signs
Of tell-tale disintegrations. He surmised,
'The trouble is that men like me
Expect to be taken seriously.'

– Convictus et combustus –

Aginthorpe had heard a rumour though
It was too early in the day to believe it.
The Turcotte woman's new piety? A passing sensation.
Then again, if to hypostatize on one's knees
Was the gift of grace, why quibble? So bc it,
Whether or no what was fellated
Should be construed as an object of worship.

– This is the way we brush our teeth
and shave our chin and shave our chin –

Yes, the reading of scripture involved
an optical illusion –
It is to say the kingdom within one,
Gone out of oneself, came beetling back
Through the organs of sight, the good book
a lens.

– Ta da. Te tum.

'Spirit is continuity –
   It is at all points contiguous,' said Aginthorpe
As he formed on his body
   An enclave of garb and raiment.

For no other reason but that we are alone
   In a crowd, in a marriage, in a frivolous game
And time remains the sum of our days,
Aginthorpe would go out.
He'd wear his best and most eternal
   Kouros-like smile, his qualities
Stuck to him like a dossier, his mind forever looping
      on its runs
   With the austere verbs of Heraclitus,
With the caustic tenderness of a Tennessee waltz.

      – This is the way we go out the door,
         out the door, out the door

WITH FEATHERS ON THE BRAIN –

: :

There are people who inspire action,
   Who fill voids with sacred energy.
And then there are those who will insist
      that stasis,
   Stillness, absolute quiescence
Is the only conduct proper for the soul,
And let the world go hang.
Aginthorpe, leaning neither to one nor the other,
      leaned into the wind.

– *Well, the mind is paradox* –

And now and then, a chance word, chance stimulus
  Triggers the certainty
That the failure one is the investiture of
  Is so much more than one imagines,
And one is the idiot of one's knowledge.

And then America, old smoke-belcher, swings around
  A bend in the river of time
To the fanfare of a republic:
  The slaves, the whores, the white-gloved gamblers,
The sleepy sense of history. America administers, carves,
    parcels out, stalemates – *it's an experiment. R&D.*

Even so, amen.

Use to God

Cowering in the cave,
Elijah on the run –

His use to God used up
Now that he'd routed Ahab's dreamers

But not the power of Ahab's queen
To hunt him down and have his head –

Surveyed the remainder of his life
and pitied it.

And either he would open his eyes once more
And begin to command the darkness

And find every object in his sight
In its proper design and place

Or he'd dive back into sleep
Like a swimmer in reverse,

That is, as a fugitive going under
So as to come up for air.

Magic Tricks

Always pulling up by the ears
  Pink-eyed rabbits from a hat,
Aginthorpe was always assigning
  To each skittish product of his magic
A philosophy, a religion, a politics
    by way of stratagems –
  He'd get tangled in this sleight of hand,
Gentleman of another Genesis,
  Muttering to himself beneath the oaks
      of a stony frontier.

One lives to live, to stay alive,
  But if a newlywed on his wedding night
In a working-class district of the neolithic
  Let go politics, death and taxes,
Drank champagne from a satin pump,
Why shouldn't we relax our grip
  And collapse upon one another
    in a paroxysm of giggles?

    – Until midway in life, the straight road lost,
      the path of fatalism is an easy path –

Aginthorpe, looking for his reflection
  In every gleaming surface on the street,
Found, instead, in a dull window,
  Notice of a discount flight
    to the island of Majorca –
He filed that away in his bean, he a perpetual
  King of the Bean, saturnalian, useless.

He was no one's scion, really.
He was no offshoot of a home-grown dynasty.
He was no Mr Bank of America.

He was no silver-hair surgeon, no crew-cut manager
    of a fast-food franchise.

He was no wild-eyed anarchist
    looking for the barricades.

He was no peer to academic perversions all the while sipping
  The month's special buy in wine
    at his fiftieth – all the while weighing out
The tribute bouquets in their tons.

CEO of his own downtrodden industry –
  The distribution-works of self – Aginthorpe had no hankering
To climb Mount Everest – had no maddening itch
  To jump from an airplane –

Had no backyard patio, had no Studebaker in the garage –
  No daughter to launch into the arms of a drug addict.

For now
  A window's showcase evening gowns,
A gallery's snowy landscape
  Artsy in its gilded frame –
The tiny bells he induced to tinkle
  As he entered some emporium
With absolutely no intention
  Of purchasing anything ...
All that was him, twenty per cent reduced.
And there were feathers on his brain,
  Those of a dilettante and a savage.

But then the next shop over (purveyor of books,
      cheerful books, dire books, gothic tracts devoted to
      the future of the bookwriting species),
And the opening salvo of a hopeful fiction
   That would be life as life really is
Assaulted his innate sense of gravity.

Aginthorpe added his thumb to the novel's frontispiece.
A clerk lipped at the computer.
It was as though lip could make the difference –
   As though one requires the machine
To remind one that one is born of a woman
   And a philanderer, is flesh, is more or less mortal
      and so, insufficient
For even the simplest of life's tasks.

And in between the trumpet blasts
   Inside Aginthorpe's throbbing head,
The pages of this book now tasted sweet
      and that book now like bitter gall.

Indeed, of further visions given the man,
   The most perplexing surely was
The sight of the elect at every trough,
   Dining on evil's condiments, the mystery of God
Winding down, a stench of fire everywhere,
   The table of literacy strewn with gaudy bowls
And vulgar candlesticks
      and other apparatus inviting Armageddon.

Even so, amen.

Aginthorpe back on the street, ready with a quip
  So as to defuse every hostile encounter
    with his fellow beings –
This coward, snob, elitist
  Just happened to forget
The ambience to which he was part.
It is to say that as he held out his hand
  To complete his rebuff to the works he beheld –
What with those testaments to spiritual suicide
  Doing their dog and pony show
Behind a plate-glass shield, a passerby slapped a coin on his palm,
    on his face mute pity.

    – Who says crime doesn't pay? –

Then a Dalmatian – exquisite, privileged – lifted leg, let rip
  On a dormant flower bed.
More trickle-down … more empire, and,
A day of rough and ready hours
  Was going to the dogs.

: :

Aginthorpe walked into a place
  As though it were home and he owned it –
And it was the Prague Café, and he sat against the wall.

    – Peasantry was painted on a vertical surface
      and so were edibles –

Yes, as long as someone somewhere dined
      on beets, on cabbage rolls, on veal and spätzle,
   As long as the dish of sliced cucumbers had
Its dressing, its ceremonial streak of spice,
   Then one could speak
Of a certain stability, a certain coherence

   In the random dispensations of all the hatreds
And the wilful baptisms of all the loves.

I'll sit and be what life's for: rotter, whinger, omnivore,
   Let waitress, all jewel and leg, bring me thin bowl of feed....

'Have You Been Served?'

And the oil and the vinegar, the salt and the pepper
  Sang each their hosannah to the beauty of women
    and the wisdom of old men.

Oil: 'How red your lips are!'
Vinegar: 'How pearly your smile!'
Salt: 'Such limpid pools, your eyes!'
Pepper: 'Prosit!'

Once in Bolsena, so Aginthorpe recalled –
  The cannelloni mouldy, the chicken dry,
The proprietor sick of tourists,
    (the wine, thank heaven, potable) –
Etruscan bones and Roman villas
    at the lake's bottom
Marked the time. The rustling of the leaves of oaks
  Blistered the vision of the eye
    in the way time adheres to time.

Tedeschi a la due!

In a bar in Barcelona, Aginthorpe sat and read
  Trollope's *He Knew He Was Right,* the bookmark a bit of herb.
He'd look up now and then and catch,
  Through a swirling haze of smoke,
Some old anti-fascist's lizard eye
  Rendering the TV absurd – that history of WW II
Going around like influenza.
The meatballs unspectacular, the sherry humdrum,
  Aginthorpe's introspection cheesy and rank ...

    – 'Have you been served?' –

What? Am I a bump on a log? Hunchback, mangy dog?

'Goulash, please, a parsley sprig – once known as crispum.
And a Diet Coke.'

'Dobře.'

'Don't mention it.'

Once, Aginthorpe – a sort of man
  People tend to be put off by
For a certain lack of productivity –
  Dreamed a fig tree, and that was labour.
How, frantically, it waved its branches –
  How it used its body language in the wind –
Was terrified, was paralysed
  From fear of the word *withered*
And the Christ of the parables
    and the dumb disciples.

A singularity of one crowding a space,
  Aginthorpe wholly within himself asked,
'Did it happen or is it just a myth?
That Jackie took the arm of de Gaulle and said,
"J'ai lu *Les Fleurs du Mal,*
    avez-vous lu *Huck Finn?*"'

Once in a revolving restaurant
   High above a city's lights
That picked at the hills like blameless vultures –
   Aginthorpe explained a poem to poets,
The hair on the back of his neck bristling.

'It's the simplest of recognition scenes, tear-jerker
      of the purest kind
Without need of Red Army Chorus,
   Mormon Tabernacle Choir,
And a parade of refugees to enhance the pathos:
   Argus wags tail, Argus dies, Odysseus weeps.
Why is it so difficult?

'To tell you the truth, I dislike dining,
   Especially at some anointed evening hour,
      with critics, with NATO secretaries,
With members of sub-committees.

'Oh, I frequent the place for other satisfactions:
   That the maître d' takes my coat,
That he asks after my health
   And seats me out of danger.
      It's a game we play.

‘Here I may imagine the Bach-playing Steiner
   Saying, even as a grisly afterthought,
Rome is a dank hole,
   Marcello disagreeing … saying, well, what did that roué say? Something
                                                                                                    about
Where it is that one is safe.

‘Perhaps my Corinna, my Stella, my Cleopatra,
      on this very night
In a town much like any other,
   Will spread her immortal legs
For yet another buffoon like me.
She can’t help but like
   What it is in her that she can’t help.
Pass the salt.’

And in this way, in the Prague Café,
   Aginthorpe would be as commonplace
As a chair, a vine, a tourist poster,
   A napkin tucked in his shirt –
And he parted the soup with a spoon,
   And with his tongue he soldered
Some hot and limitless dread of complications
      to his palate.

Tryst

There's always drama in entrances,
   Action, lights and camera,
      and enough fool behaviour
To confirm every leftover lover's
      worst suspicions.

      – She walked into the café –

Design or fate – who's to say?
Destiny is a word that begins with *d.*
Destiny in the mind looks for trouble,
   As it does in the soul and the feckless body –
It's a regular search party.

: :

The Turcotte woman scanned the place
   With an air of competence,
And though Aginthorpe caught her eye,
   And she caught his and dropped it,
      she had other ideas, expecting a tête-à-tête, no less,
   With some other of the difficult sex
      Who would be half her age.

It's to say that, before she spied her date,
   Aginthorpe saw on the Turcotte woman's face
      a worried look,
An
   I-could-be-his-mother
Kind of look –

Poetry up for grabs in her long-legged stride
   And a quarrel she would provoke in Aginthorpe:

That her very own Hippolytus
   Was venally devoid of character
And much too sensitive
   For a mature seductress: all that metal fastened to
Lips and lobes, he the centre of a universe.

      – Ah, real life –

It was the very thing, that old inspiring fetish
   Of the early movie-makers
Who, obsessed with epic sweep, cranked away
   Furiously on their machines,
Chased after galloping horses in earth-rattling battle scenes,
   Ogled nude dancers, resurrected
      Casanova's leer,
Quoted Victor Hugo, something to the effect
   Of history's wheel and whom it crushes.

      – But not a word about the Knicks in the Garden,
         the CIA in Baghdad, or: *Ich bin ein Berliner!* –

Well, Aginthorpe imagined how it should have gone –
   He piled it on –
Took the Turcotte woman's coat, drew her out a chair.

      – He bussed this Turcotte on the cheek –

And if, in Aginthorpe's fevered inner prose,
   A wary shadow swiftly rose,
Shark-like, from her inner deeps,
And feasted on her eyes' sweet nature,
   Harmed a round, pretty, sporting face
(while tenderly he squeezed the hand
   of a female without parallel),

Well, it were better to have been warned
to keep to his table and keep off hers
Than be cut forever from the herd.

Aginthorpe fought to keep food down –
His was a heroic effort,
While she, so near, so far, took off – one by one –
Each finger's leather sheath of glove.
In the light of the sun that in winter had
no weight or substance
Save for what she imparted to it,
The Turcotte woman lined up her boy lover
In the cross-hairs of her wants –
Lined up the spent option ten feet over
As an embarrassment she didn't need
just at that second.

Yes, a line held in suspension between her lips
That one might say had traced a smile,
Spoke not only for all the ghosts of love
But for every realized moment.

'How am you,' she used to ask, getting down to cases,
To the business of being vulnerable.

'I are vile, of course,' Aginthorpe used to answer,
Abusing the verb so as to appear indifferent
To a magnificence shot through
with threadbare sympathy.

'Yes, I are as vile as one can be
Who crept out of a cheerless womb
Into a household of stinking virtue,
Pedigree, you know, my nemesis.'

Aginthorpe used to succeed with this chatter,
   Established himself as a callow gent,
So much so

That as one sentence would lead to another –
   As one six-billionth of a collective
Would seek its opposite infinitesimal part
   In the mass,
Would form a random shape
   And the shape was hopeless,
Often, this old flame of his, colleague in lust,
   Rising, would draw herself up
To her full stature, a stark dream-figure
   In the blaze of the sun that in winter lacks weight,
      and shake him loose.

: :

The civilities exchanged, the Turcotte woman
      now leaned forward
So as better to hear the best
      of a private schooling in her find:
The longish hair, the brooding, egoistical eyes.

Aginthorpe thought: 'What? Is this youth
   Of a terrible sincerity a philosopher, too? Oh my.
Will it rise and we hold our peace
   While it gyrates now to the brass,
Now to the marimba section
   Of *Being and Nothingness,*
And she wonder
   How on earth she can follow the dance?'

Across the distance into which the sun
  Was sinking deep mine shafts,
This sun that in winter has no
  Weight or substance, Aginthorpe heard:

'Perhaps I can clarify. Bluebirds are not blue,
    but I'll grant you
  They're blue in the ways that matter to us.
Mrs Turcotte, let's fornicate.'

And immediately upon hearing mention
    of this proposition, Aginthorpe saw:

fornicatus, p. p. of fornicari

And then heard:

'In your vaulted chamber
  On a pile of plush pillows.'

A prickly, nasty solitary
  Gazing with infinite sight
Across the spinning disc of the universe,
  The nothingness at its edge
Sucking up all the matter
  And so, increasing the velocity
Of the universe's stretching out,
  Aginthorpe in his mind met head-on
The young stripling's discount thought-system
    and counter-postulated,

‘Blue? Is that all? Is that all there is to say about birds?
Though their flying look like freedom, the little rotters
   Are pretty well doomed. Death follows their drudgery.’

That the world is administered, yes,
   Is carved and parcelled out
In endlessly varying shapes and sizes –
   It’s stalemate all the time. . . .

      – The Turcotte woman said, ‘Bluebirds, eh?
        Lovely things.’ –

      – ‘Aha!’ chortled Aginthorpe,
          ‘she’s not one to stand for nonsense.’ –

But in his mind even his heroes were failing him,
   They smatterings, anyway, of dust:
Petronius, Theocritus, Machado de Assis.

          We were interrupted by the sound of a carriage.
          A slave announced that it was Baroness X.
          Virgilia consulted me with her eyes.

      – Where was the pagan justice:
          that the best man gets the best girl? –

Ruffians, Rape and Riches

As though occupying an atoll in a sea of them,
   Aginthorpe at his table heard:

'Your father's demented? I'll go you one better. Mine with a gun as red
   As a lollipop (it was a toy that squirted water),
Pulled a heist – well, he almost did
   Back when he had ambitions
And banks were more convenient.
Mother would say, "He won't grow up.
Tell me again why I married him.
Drinking rotgut – living in a shack
   By the seat of our pants ..."'

Aginthorpe saw the speaker,
   Her hair hot fuchsia pink, nails blue, leggings orange,
      combat footwear parade-ground-ready.
She was a citizen of one of Saturn's moons
   Or maybe Nova Scotia, here on a cultural exchange.

Heard:

Pah! Poetry is useless.

Once Aginthorpe dreamed in fits and starts
   The chat-filled pages of a Renaissance scribbler,
Could see the ornate fountains of a garden where,
To the sound of splashing wine,
   To the sight of darkening stone,
He conversed with a finger-wagging humanist,
   Synthesizer of Christ and pagan.

You can't imagine a Borgia
As House Speaker in the U.S. of A.?

Well, what makes you undoes you –
What's gained is loss – the difference spells
perpetual twilight.

Heard:

'You're much too naïve, my man. Ruffians, rape and riches –
Now that's how you flesh out a thriller –
That's how you make oodles of cash,
That's how you get invited
To play a game of tennis.
Leave literature to the critic –
The one deserves the other.'

Heard:

The aristocratic bias
In the voice of this interlocutor.

In the café, Aginthorpe – an island in a sea of troubles – reasoned.
He had never been to Prague, city famous for its alchemists,
For its episodes of extreme religiosity,
for its clocks, its intellectual traditions.
Even so, he could suppose
That the Turcotte woman,
Gone with her Johnny-dear
To perhaps drink whisky in a bar,
Was an institution with antecedents
As when the affections are secure
But that every love has its
grade, rating, seal –

As when a man believes all cities have
  Their glories and horrors and in-crowds
At pimp-infested restaurants,
  But that every love is stamped
With its date of expiry.

I am less than real – I want nothing real
  Because that's the way it is – it's a daily referendum.
If Socrates picked a quarrel with Athens,
  At least, he was a law-abiding misfit.
Whereas I, I'm not even on the radar.
So bring on the floozies – better that
  Than collusion in spurious commitment,
Than exchanges in bed of immortal ideas
    between idiots.

  – 'Well, that did it,' thought Aginthorpe
    on a cold, cold day in January –

Then a tickle in his throat, an itch, a crumb of something
  Caused him to spew.

Dragons breathe fire, squids squirt ink,
  Whales blow, lions roar –
Elephants trumpet, snakes hiss
And camels spit –
  Warblers warble, geese honk –
Even the sons of senators sneeze
  With whatever their noses ingest –
In fact, most creatures are given
  To auditory excrescences,
But Aginthorpe, he just lost control.

– Mortified, Aginthorpe staged
   a show of penitence –

And reaching for the serviette
  The man's typhoon swept away from her,
A woman signalled her disgust
  To the inclement weather source –
Aginthorpe admired the arm
  That belonged to this legatee
Of a recent wealth-event.

– But she had no more time for dalliance
   than snow in May has for the mud beneath it –

Cheque please, waitress, and water –
  I am thirsty and worse, without honour.
Change and its works, hardening in mind after mind –
  How can one live with the pressure?

Ballroom Champion

A ballroom champion on an icy street,
  The contest prize overrated,
The hours leased
  By the usual threats, by the usual promises,
The usual honeymoons
  With which pernicious people
Invest pernicious mental products,
    the weapon of choice
  Hindsight,
Moral ascendancy the sacred ground, Aginthorpe put
  The debacle in the café behind him.

    – Besides, his enemies have no predators
      natural, unnatural or otherwise –

        Alone with Marcella, I loosed all the desperation
          that had been locked in my heart. . . .

Still, a lunch consumed, that tête-à-tête observed,
  An affirmation of self, worth and function had,
And my!
  He was now almost human, one of those
Tough, spiritual beings hurrying along,
    soul a tango,
Or something all angular and all hauteur
  Hard by the steel and glass prospects
Of wealth manufacture – Aginthorpe sucked
    on the frozen air.

– Memory shapes all the corroding fears –

It's hard to believe but heaven takes
  No pleasure in the intangibles,
Heaven crowded with Midwest co-ops,
  Silent majorities,
Death the thing rich in properties
    of the sentient mind.

It is to say that, to warm himself,
  Aginthorpe ducked into a church that was near at hand,
Looked down the nave until
  The passenger on the cross
Was in his sight –

And it seemed to Aginthorpe that his own lips moved –
  It seemed to him that his own thought thought:

Aginthorpe, you dog,
  Conversion is beside the point.

– Well, the place wasn't the Della Salute, no dead rats afloat
    in the Grand Canal –

Even so – yes – he'd phone her now,
  Beg forgiveness now of the Turcotte woman, inform her
Of his churchly episode, watch this bear fruit –

Say anything to her,
  Gain admittance to her bed,
Get cachet among her limbs
    (Aginthorpe an amateur remarkably inspired) –

Smooch mouth, bite ear, suck big toe –
  Three categorical statements in a row –
Hear sweet, raucous laughter –
  Take her body as for granted as she would –
    compelling arrangement –

And afterwards,
                go for ice cream.

    – But don't write anything nasty about Ferrara
      or the Estes will come and haunt you –

'Hello. Aginthorpe here. Look, my darling,
  It seems to me …
What? *Don't darling you?*
What? You have a visitor?
Anyway, as I was saying,
  Just as Keats saw through beauty
And found all was dark,
  So I've seen through death
And discovered light: *my sweet, you.*
What?
I'm no copy cat.'

'... can't you give your boy wonder a quarter
   And send him to the movies?'

For these things come out of nowhere
   To confound, to harass, to militate
Against one's pride of self and sense of place –

That divided between sleep and waking,
   The sensation almost exquisite
As when one's certain one's alive
   But a question nags the air –

In what illumination the dark may give
   Tonguing a conscience like the flickering
Tongue of a snake, here's the Christ in prayer –
   There are Herod's construction projects,
The gold plating of which reflects
   Moonlight and intensity.

The Turcotte Woman in Her Element

Say what you want about sex,
  That it was always the frontier –
That trading in trinkets of mind and desire,
  One bargained but mostly cheated,
And your point will be honoured
  In some badlands saloon.

That even in the bedroom sentries,
  Commando units, palace guards,
With knives and spears, automatic weapons,
  Followed the movements of smugglers
And pedlars of bogus medicines
  Operating among the tribal and the tribeless
Who, in their turn, tagged after armies
    with irascible, portable deities.

That the frontier was always the bedroom, yes indeed –
  It was the attempt at décor,
The struggle not only to accommodate
  A plethora of factions to order
But the colour of the curtains
  To the shade of rug on the floor.

Yes, in a diary, one was assigned a letter:
  'Today, *A* – that louse – said he adored me
And would kiss me from head to toe
  With one or two detours.
    Promises, promises.'

Well, Nietszche said a man will sacrifice everything,
  Every life happiness, in his lust for power.
Not Aginthorpe.

That governorship, presidency, sultanate,
  The helm of some corporate yacht –
None of it mattered, for, as a writer wrote:

Apparently, Virgilia was beginning to tire of me.

Besides, the Turcotte woman had been dubious
  When Aginthorpe was on the blower to her:

'You spiritual? In your dreams!
If I told Mariott I had an episode,
  It was to see if it would annoy him.
It made him want to hump me, he got so excited....
Where? At your party. On your couch.
Imagine it: a mountain of Jell-O on my body,
  Boobs jostling like a nervous pig's –
To pinch an image from your Theocritus.
All right. I'll get rid of the young genius.
Against my better judgement,
    we'll discuss this.'

: :

And Aginthorpe would buy her a bouquet of forgiveness,
        three posies each
For art, religion and science,
    For each breakthrough in a contest category,
For just the right timely thing
    That would appeal to her bluestocking sense of progress –

And clutching these flowers with all his might,
    Hoping, all the while, for mild crosswinds,
He'd parachute down on her milky-white bosom
    To carry out a proper task of Zeus.

And if words and gifts couldn't win her,
    If dragon-slaying and other quests
Left her indifferent,
    If riches failed, if rough treatment
Only bored the woman, if a gentle stroking
    Of her chestnut tresses
Never ceased to get on her nerves,
    He'd ask what would,
What was likely to meet with her approval.

: :

And if it is fashion that benignly stuffs
    The void between sex and loneliness
With its cheerful, positive, forward-thinking
        here-ness and now-ness

so that most moments are untruths, a clutching at straws

Certainly, her address was fashionable,
  The intimate brownstones, the narrow tree-lined streets.
And certainly she was most in her element
    when she mugged
Wolfgang Amadeus,
  Hammered Haydn,
Diminished the blues
  By dint of an absence of whisky and smoke –
But never mind – she wasn't hard to look at,
    willowy, of grace.

    – She managed to fit in Aginthorpe, her schedule a busy one –

Lot and Spindle

And though born by lot and then turned by the spindle
Of circumstance – the stars intent upon their acts,
The soul on its task – one is not rubber-stamped.
Plotinus wrote something like this.

But you know how it is: a man will believe,
When he has been around long enough,
That he has seen most people – has known every greed
for good and lust for bad –
And he'd be a pompous ass were he to bruit
the gossip about.
A man, acquainted even with his own antics,
Will persuade himself he has an inkling
Of the Circuit of the All – so best go and get a drink
and settle down.

So Aginthorpe, as it were, loved – the man, so to speak, set right
By the Turcotte woman
(who'd mother all men
over and above their protests), left her shaking her head
And swearing: *never again* –
And in the street,
Aginthorpe stuck up his arm and hailed a cab.

: :

Fishtailing in the snow, a taxi stopped.
It seemed a beast, some cousin to a shark,
The driver a being Aginthorpe had never
clapped eyes on before.

– The soul had nowhere to go but to the body, an endless difficulty
for the ancient philosophers –

Rightly or wrongly, certain men of these times
  Will believe it is of shabby stuff
The soul is made, and everything out there:
  Grey tree and shrub and shivering bird,
  The brick and the steel and the glass
    reinforce
The shoddy architecture, the second-rate material
  Of desire, *and talk is silly, action futile,*
    and silence unbearable.

'Did you hear the one about the polar bear
    who goes into a bar?' asked the driver.

'No,' thought Aginthorpe, *but did you hear*
  This about Mrs Schlempenmeier, children's author –
How she, thin and stooped, at a feast dispirited,
  Picked at her chicken and gulped her wine –
Then took my hand in her cold hand,
  Her knuckles a range of snow-capped volcanoes –
  Then squeezed my palm as I worried much –
Then said into my ear (as I went rigid),
  That her soul was dead – it had been a vanity
    all along.

    – I answered her: 'Really? No, it's impossible' –

'Yes,' thought Aginthorpe, *and there's more, so much more:*
  The sea's calm surface, the feeding frenzy beneath,
Just as reason had nowhere to go
  But to the body....

: :

You know how it is: sometimes it has to be said
      how things are: at Marriot's place the air
Was thick with hash. Wine breathed, and Marriot was
      immense and pleased with himself.

And the heel of young Priscilla's dirty sock
      Was a peepshow.
Her pupils were black when her eyes weren't shut
      And dreamy, her smile glassy, chin anxious.

      – Mariott said, 'I am, as you can see, mentoring' –

The robe he wore, red and gold-trimmed,
   Embellished with star-configurations,
Was a hyperbole, was as hyperbolic
   As the timeless boulevards and heavy foliage
Of summer, a season for which
      Aginthorpe suddenly ached.

Shock Therapy

Aginthorpe preoccupied, slumped on the couch,
  One leg crossed over the other,
And he caught a barrage of Mariott words
  That would state most cases
By the light of Mariott prescience,
  Mariott waggling his jewelled fingers.
Young Priscilla, eyes much too bright, exuded sex, gave off wisdom
  Like the sun does flares, a sock worn through at the heel.

Said Mariott, with a patrician nod at the girl,
  'Her children can expect a term of life
Twice that of ours – consider it.
Boredom. The idea of passion absurd.
Consciousness dimmed in self-defence.
Perhaps the young dumb down for a reason.'

    – 'I mean,' said Mariott, 'how many times can one watch
        Boris Godunov?' –

And now Aginthorpe, with his eyes, took in this Priscilla:
  The bare shoulders, the patchwork jeans, the potent breasts,
The heart-breaking attempt to come by serenity.
Just a child.
Just a child.
A brat.

    – 'I mean,' said Mariott, 'what's there to know? Observe the spider
        drain the fly of its juice – there's your eloquence.' –

And Aginthorpe, with his eyes, took in this Priscilla:
The chewed nails, the chipped polish, the bad posture,
The heart-breaking attempt to come by the grail
Of some authenticity.
Just a babe.
Just a babe.
Jailbait.

– 'I mean,' said Mariott, 'does nature give a fig
for anyone past the age of baby-making?' –

Aginthorpe, with his eyes, took in this Priscilla
and was repelled.

– 'I mean,' said Mariott, 'that human freedom
is nature's indifference' –

Priscilla slid off the chair. She gathered herself,
And with the unexpected regality of a queen,
Approached Aginthorpe for a light –
A smirk on her face, she guided
His unaccountably nervous hand
to her cigarette.

– Mariott, immense, seemed pleased with himself –

'Well,' thought Aginthorpe, 'the mind is paradox,
Eternity repose, time something else.'

What? Am I an evolutionist? Let the melancholy say what they will,
life is sweet.

And Mariott relit his pipe – Priscilla, reseated,
   Shoulders hunched, looked the very part
      of girlishness. She swayed, eyes unnaturally bright.
It was as though the clock were not ticking....
Mariott sucked – Aginthorpe inwardly
   Dictated a note to Turcotte:

Madame,

If I were a gentleman, which I'm not,
   I'd serve you notice of my loss of faith (and so, cut my losses).
Still, wishing to resume my studies,
   And because it requires my wherewithal,
I let you know that I will curtail my visits.
In other words, allow me to quit before you fire me.
I wish you every happiness.

      – P.S. Isn't that your daughter
            the Mariott fellow is messing with? –

The Mystical Masseuse

I wasn't always the man I seem to be, Priscilla:
Whinger, rotter, omnivore. What happened?
Let me explain it this way.
Let me describe a woman – not your mother.
She advertised healing – I fell for it. Here's the tale.

How, over the course of an hour, in a session,
To the sob of mood music, not with her body but with her mind
She pummelled my tender parts –
Thrashed me, minced me, this Amazon.

Yes, with her ancient, hard-won methods, she possessed
the pizazz, as it were,
To make one sane, creative, absurdly rich –
But her physique, without the schooling,
Her physique stunning to behold, would have sufficed
To put me on the right side of history.

– Her long hair was dense with curls,
white teeth gleaming self.... What was I thinking? –

Well, I had resources, too, ones I'd quite forgotten,
The likes of Ovid and Horace to back
my mounting sense of rebellion.
Had any of us then an ounce of strength
We might have reversed the flow of health,
For she was game, devoted, principled, tireless.

No, I can't deny the pleasure of the relief that followed,
Wars of religion and territory
A dim memory now, old evils
Dropping away like dead skin.
Rouge pranced on her lips.
Never has nature fashioned
A more devastating egotist!

So now I was seasoned by her lights – I was almost prepared to tread along
The new paths of righteousness.
'You'll soon be human,' she announced,
'Nearly fit for human company.'
It would seem I was a kind of panda.
She arched her eyebrows at me reconstituted
Lest I doubt her capacities.

Shoulders thrown back, breasts high and proud,
She stood tall for values.
My posture diffident, the sad fact remains,
I always lapse. Immediately, I did so.
I lit out of her boudoir. I'm still running.

So now Priscilla, while Mariott,
Immense and massive, dozes,
I'll leave – I really must get back
To 'Plotinus Against the Gnostics'.
Don't be in too much of a rush, my dear:
Life will seek you out.

The Turcotte Woman's Letter to Aginthorpe

DEAR *A*,
It has been many weeks
Since we last communicated.
You asked, 'Who, between man and woman,
    is the more ferocious
When it comes to forgiving but not relenting?'
I say, 'I can't say.'
I hope all's well.

Dear *A*,
It is April. Well then, let's have it:
The birds, the budding, the changing wind –
The sun's pale plumage suggestive
    of the heat to come.

Dear *A*,
It is April
And it's snowed and snowed
    in biblical amounts.

Dear *A*,
I must say no life but mine concerns me now –
I drink less – I read much. There is a catechism
With all its quaint *Thou shalt nots*
Interdictions to which Clough, in his time, appended …
    well, it went something like this:

    Thou shalt not kill except when provoked extremely….

Dear *A*,
Let it please you to know
I have removed from my diaries
The pages in which you figure.
That to life's vagaries I have returned you.

Dear *A*,
You had said:
  'A gentleman does not fault a lady
And leave himself unexamined.'
What of *a rotter, a whinger, an omnivore?*

Dear *A*,
Poor you. So hopeless.

Dear *A*,
It is April. I will bring to Mariott
Chicken soup. He's sick – he's lonely,
    most discontented.
His body disgusts me – his mind excites me,
And if you think I cannot partition
    anyone like this, remember
I am a woman, all of a piece, entitled
To enjoin this darkness of ours
    with my caprice.
I define men as creatures who can, after all, love
    but who doubt it.

Dear *A*,
It is April.
I read and I read.
I would like to have been
Helen, mother of Constantine.

Dear *A*,
Strike that. It is April. Only that.

Dear *A*,
Last night, a jingle invaded my mind –
It was this: *Have some pity for poor Dunlevy,*
He got tired of becoming....

Dear *A*,
I would want, I think, the thoughts of the Apostle John
Who was struck dumb after he wrote what he wrote.

Dear *A*,
Perhaps you expect to hear of my plans –
Quite frankly, there are none.
It's April. I read much.

Dear *A*,
I do not gloat that I am rid of you.
Why blame a man who, in his mind, thought he loved?

Dear *A*,
Let nature go hang.

Dear *A*,
I really do believe
God is indifferent to us, and yet,
Every once in a while, I sense in me
Something not wholly me –
And this is the last I'll speak of it.

Dear *A*,
It is April.
It is April.
There's that, at least.

Darling *A*,
You should wander.
It seems to me you're restless.

Dear *A*,
Nowhere to go?
So sorry.

Dear *A*,
I pity you.

Dear *A*,
Love, *M*.

Aginthorpe on the Divan

It was the room's only bit of furniture,
  The divan inlaid with mother-of-pearl
Around which Aginthorpe walked three times
  Like a dog preparing the ground
    for a dog's volcanic sleep.

    – The wood was cypress, painted black –

The light of the neon that filled the room
  With the commerce of the evening
Was like the polish of a jug of cold lemonade
  Sparkling with ice cubes on a hot afternoon,
    clouds building, voices subdued.

And the shishing and the shushing in Aginthorpe's ears
  Was the sound of tires on the street,
The traffic passing by in waves –
  Monotonous, impersonal.

I am not to be pitied.
Who's to be pitied?
No one's to be pitied. Not really. Not in the grand scheme of things …

Heard:

'Shut up, bitch!'

Aginthorpe fingered the pendant
  That was the shape of a crescent moon
Attached to a chain around his neck –
  It was silver – it was a memento
Of long-dead harvest times
  And the words of them that no one recalled
Or would ever, again, remember.

It was nothing, really, this antique,
This curio, curiosity-piece
That one might idly caress,
The mind slowed to a snail's
headlong rush.

I breathed as she breathed and smelled her hair,
Idea and disaster in permanent fruition,
Elysium as dark a rest.

– Aginthorpe shut his eyes –

And it was the wrong time of the year for seeing,
as he did, the leaves falling yellow and red,
For seeing, as he did,
The wind in this way
And the darkening sky.

Maybe for the wife of that president,
Maybe for Keats at the seaside,
There was reason to pity them just as one pities
the tribesman caught up in yet another famine.

'Clearly, it has been no exaggeration – the place evil,
Every stone, every blade of grass,
Every sap-pumping tree,
Every dull, tiny bird,
Every factory-moulded product,
Every amber, distinctive liqueur
A malaise through no fault of their own.'

– So Aginthorpe speculated it through –

Now music might have been good to hear
  For no good earthly reason.

I brought her wine and tiger lilies
  And she put pot roast on the table.

Aginthorpe, born on Truman's watch,
  Could not have known how little that mattered –
That is, his bloody birth,
  As, just then, some defence stipend was being squeezed
    from a Republican Congress.

Love, you may have been a woman.
Or you may have been the Christ.
You might have been all the pagan jesters
  Who distracted every mean court
From life's ennui, from death's emptiness –
  And you may have been a poet
Such as is always pitiable –
  To proclaim that the sound, the meaning, the rhythms of words,
Like the breathing of a tiger in the bush,
  Can ever disperse the evils of the night –
But Love, you were never the world.

Rotter, whinger, omnivore, Aginthorpe said aloud,
  'Tell me, is there a point in the distance
Where, when you arrive at it
  The silliest of wounds fall away,
The bleariest of eyes see unimpeded,
  And all's mirth in a blessed house?'

What? Are you nuts?

Once Aginthorpe dreamed that through pretty shards of glass
He saw the craters of the moon,
And the path to the shining rock
Was an expressway to knowing
everything
Though it'd been a road of sheep,
Goats and shepherds.

– No more distances, please,
knowledge intensifies loneliness –

God, take me. Don't want me, then have
These, my most prized possessions: 1953 Buick grille,
Respighi, Beethoven, Mahler LP's,
Those church windows in the garage
That cost a pretty penny.
Clap your red-hot hands on it, God,
And leave me alone.

– Aginthorpe lay still, a portrait in the making –

Once, under the scrutiny of a mom and a dad,
Your boyish, much too eager hand
Perhaps betrayed its culpability, trembling as it returned
To the scene of an earlier intent, the desert of which
Was now to bloom forth
With a cool, white corsage, the prom at eight.

– The moon was full, the night cold –

The universe, they say now, is flat
   And is forever stretching out.
Be that as it may, Aginthorpe could imagine
      what one might find

Should one drift into Africa,
      and the sun will explode.

The universe, they say, is not curved at all,
   And we may never go to a place
Only to return where we started from –
   And there's always something
      lurking in the cupboard.

Have some pity for poor Dunlevy.
He got tired of becoming.

Aginthorpe said, 'That she took me into the ark of her bed,
   That she laid her hands on me
And I on her, and there was every pleasure,
   And then birds appeared
To announce landfall,
   Was it to our advantage? Did it give us an edge
      in species maintenance?
Did we have to roll the dice?'

: :

Enough. Aginthorpe sighed and this time truly fell
      into a fathomless sleep.

Acknowledgements

'Hypatia' has appeared in *PN Review*, 134.

The author acknowledges the financial assistance of the Canada Council for the Arts.

100%
Beef
FRANKS
Jamaican Style
Beef PATTIES
Hot or Sweet
Delicious Italian

MARY HARMAN

Norm Sibum has been writing and publishing poetry for over thirty years. Born in Oberammergau in 1947, he grew up in Germany, Alaska, Utah and Washington. He has published several volumes of poetry in Canada; his last two books, *The November Propertius* and *In Laban's Field,* were published by Carcanet Press, Manchester, England. Sibum currently lives in Montreal.